EGYPT

by
Gail B. Stewart

CRESTWOOD HOUSE
New York

Maxwell Macmillan Canada
Toronto

Maxwell Macmillan International
New York Oxford Singapore Sydney

Library of Congress Cataloging-in-Publication Data
Stewart, Gail, 1949–
    Egypt / by Gail B. Stewart. — 1st ed.
        p.   cm. — (Places in the news)
    Summary: Examines the historical events that have shaped Egypt's destiny.
    ISBN 0-89686-744-7
    1. Egypt—History—Juvenile literature. 2. Egypt—Politics and government—1952–   —Juvenile literature.
[1. Egypt—History.] I. Title. II. Series: Stewart, Gail, 1949–   Places in the news.
DT77.S77   1992
962—dc20   91-33485

Photo Credits
Cover: AP—Wide World Photos
AP—Wide World Photos: 4, 19, 22, 24, 29, 30, 33, 34, 37, 39, 40, 41, 42, 44
The Bettmann Archive: 9, 15, 16

CRESTWOOD HOUSE

Macmillan Publishing Company
866 Third Avenue
New York, NY 10022

Maxwell Macmillan Canada, Inc.
1200 Eglinton Avenue East
Suite 200
Don Mills, Ontario M3C 3N1

Macmillan Publishing Company is part of the Maxwell Communication Group of Companies.

Produced by Flying Fish Studio

Printed in the United States of America

First Edition

10 9 8 7 6 5 4 3 2 1

CONTENTS

Rifaat el-Maghoub is shot dead when assasins open fire on his limo.

EGYPT
IN THE NEWS

"There was a solid minute of gunfire, and we could hear nothing else," sobbed a young woman. "Then all we could hear were screams and the sounds of motorcycles speeding away."

The woman was describing the tragic afternoon on Saturday, October 13, 1990. Rifaat el-Maghoub, the second-ranking official in Egypt, was murdered on the streets of Egypt's capital city, Cairo. In front of dozens of witnesses, and in spite of an armed group of bodyguards, Maghoub was shot, and his killers escaped easily.

"Under This Beautiful Blue Egyptian Sky"

Maghoub had been traveling in his chauffeur-driven black Mercedes. Another car had followed him, full of Egyptian state-security men. Like the United States, many nations guard and protect important government officials.

As Maghoub's limousine drove down a wide avenue near a 28-story luxury hotel along the Nile River, two motorcycles sped alongside. On the back of the motorcycles, behind the drivers, were men with automatic weapons. They opened fire on Maghoub's car as well as on the security car behind it.

"It was so unexpected, so strange," said an American businessman who saw the shooting from his car. "The motorcyclists pulled out these big weapons and just started spraying everything with bullets. There were brass cartridge casings all over the street—everywhere.

"We in America are used to thinking of murder as something that happens at night, in a dark alley or somewhere. But here, in full view of everyone, under this beautiful blue Egyptian sky—it doesn't make any sense at all. The whole thing still gives me nightmares."

Who's to Blame?

Egypt's president, Hosni Mubarak, called Maghoub's assassination "a detestable crime, which stooped to the lowest depths of treachery and cowardice."

U.S. President George Bush, in a statement to the press,

agreed with Mubarak. Bush said that the event was an example of "the most vile kind of terrorism."

The uppermost question in the minds of Egyptians, of course, was Who's to blame? There were several possibilities since many groups of people were anxious to assassinate an Egyptian official.

Shortly before Maghoub's murder, Egypt's government had spoken out against Saddam Hussein's invasion of Kuwait. President Mubarak had called Iraq's action "a criminal act, one which should bring shame on the government of Saddam Hussein."

Mubarak's words had startled many people. Egypt is an Arab country, as is Iraq. For many years, Arab nations have tried to be unified in their statements and their actions. Rarely has the leader of one Arab nation been openly critical of another.

But Mubarak spoke out against Iraq's aggression. He sided with the United States and other nations of the world that condemned Saddam Hussein's actions. According to some political experts, that may have been the reason behind the assassination of Maghoub.

It could have been done by Egyptians furious with Mubarak for breaking Arab solidarity. It could have been done by any one of several Arab terrorist organizations angry with Mubarak for the same reason. Because Maghoub was a longtime political friend of Mubarak, killing him would send a very direct message to the Egyptian president.

But other experts now see another possible motive for the killing. They point to deep religious differences among the people of Egypt. Most Egyptians are Muslims, who practice the faith called Islam. Many Muslims in Egypt feel threatened because their old traditions are fading out and the government is not doing anything to help.

Many Muslims are angry at Mubarak and other Egyptian officials for not adhering strictly to Islamic ideas. These Muslims are known as fundamentalists. Fundamentalist leaders have been urging rebellion and violence in recent months.

Can Maghoub's tragic death be linked to religious groups in Egypt? Or are Arab terrorist groups to blame? And what is the cause of the increasing violence and unrest that threaten Egypt today?

AN ANCIENT HERITAGE

To understand why Egypt is in the news today, it helps to learn about the origins of its problems. Egypt is one of the oldest civilizations on earth. Many of the problems in modern Egypt can be seen in the country's ancient history.

Centuries of Domination

Egypt has been one of the most important places in the Middle East for many centuries. It is considered part of the Arab world, those lands that are inhabited by people originally from the land called Arabia. In fact, Egypt has been a center of the Arab world for more than 1,400 years.

But Egypt's civilization goes back even further than that. Egypt's history can be traced back more than 4,000 years, to the time of the powerful pharaohs, or rulers. They had elegant pal-

Egypt, one of the oldest civilizations on earth

aces and priceless art fashioned in gold and precious stones. And when the pharaohs died, they were buried in tombs stocked with money and treasures.

These ancient Egyptians were religious, but their religion differed greatly from modern religions. They believed in many gods, all of whom controlled every aspect of people's lives. There was a god of war, a god of the sun, a goddess who protected the dead. These gods and goddesses were worshiped, and their priests were highly respected by all Egyptians.

The ancient history of Egypt is also a story of domination by others. Over the course of the centuries, the power of the pharaohs weakened. Invaders from across the Mediterranean Sea and from Asia came to Egypt and were pleasantly surprised at what they found. Here was a country that was mostly desert. But along the Nile River there were fertile, rich farmlands, perfect for growing food. Egypt became a sought-after nation.

Persians and Assyrians came and conquered Egypt. In 332 B.C., Alexander the Great came and took Egypt in the name of the Greek Empire. The Egyptian people changed each time a new army invaded their country. The conquerors left their marks on the language, the customs and even the religion of the Egyptians.

Religious Differences

In 30 B.C., armies from the powerful Roman Empire came to Egypt. For the next 350 years Egypt was ruled as a Roman province. The Romans used Egypt and gave very little in return. They took vast amounts of the grain grown in the lush fields near the Nile. They used this grain to feed their own people. As a result, many Egyptians went hungry.

During this time, the huge Roman Empire split into two parts: the Western Empire and the Eastern, or Byzantine, Empire. The Byzantine emperors decreed that Christianity would replace the Egyptians' own religion. The ancient temples used by the Egyptian people were ordered closed, and the holy statues of the gods and goddesses were destroyed.

The Egyptians gradually became Christian, but a different kind of Christian than their Byzantine rulers were. They were called Coptic Christians. They believed that Jesus was totally divine and was not human.

The Byzantines scoffed at this nation. To them, Jesus was both human and divine. Because the Coptic Christians had such different beliefs, they were often discriminated against and looked down upon by the Byzantines.

The Byzantine emperors weakened Egypt. Besides forcing the people to accept a religion that wasn't their own, they hurt the economy of the country. They divided the land into small communities, each ruled by a lord. The common people were powerless—their only worth was to work for the lords and pay outrageously high taxes to support the lords' lavish lifestyles.

The Coming of the Muslims

In the A.D. 7th century, when a new power invaded Egypt, the Egyptian people were not upset. They were more than willing to assist the newcomers in fighting the Byzantine armies. These newcomers were Muslims from Arabia and followed Islam.

Islam had its beginnings in the desert of Arabia early in that

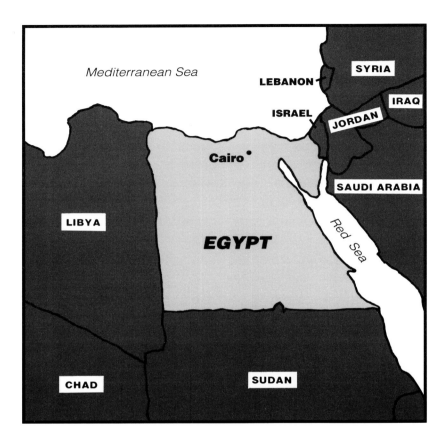

same century. A young man named Kutam was visited by the angel Gabriel. Gabriel told Kutam that he was to be the holy messenger of God. He was to devote his life to one God, called Allah, who would direct him in the proper way to live and act. And Kutam would no longer be called by his original name. From that day forward he would be called Muhammad.

During his lifetime Muhammad spread the word of his new religion. After Muhammad's death the message of Islam was carried throughout the Middle East, including Egypt.

One of the basic beliefs of Islam is that the religion must be taught to other people—whether or not they are willing to hear it! Sometimes spreading the word became quite forceful—many people became Muslims by the sword.

But in Egypt that was not the case. The Muslim warriors were surprised and relieved to find the Egyptians supportive of them. The Byzantine rulers were defeated, and in A.D. 639, Egypt became a nation ruled by Arab Muslims.

Under Muslim Rule

A great deal changed during the rule of the Arab Muslims. Unlike the Byzantine leaders, who had decreed that the Egyptians had to become Christians, the Arab rulers allowed the Egyptians to choose their own religions. The Coptic Christians, who had been scorned by the Byzantines, were given the freedom once again to believe what they chose.

Even so, many Egyptians turned to Islam, giving up Christianity. Throughout the centuries that followed, Egypt became more and more Arab and showed fewer signs of the Greek and Roman traditions that had influenced the country in the past.

Various Muslim rulers kept control of Egypt—some rulers were strong and others were weak. Then, in 1517, following a time of weak rulers, Turkish armies invaded Egypt and took control. These Turks, who called their vast realm the Ottoman Empire, were also Muslims.

However, the Ottoman culture and language were different from those of the Arabs. They had a different philosophy about governing, too. While the Arabs had contributed to Egypt's culture, the Turks only used it. They exploited its treasures and resources and sent its wealth to Constantinople (now Istanbul), the Turkish capital. The Egyptians were not receptive to these Turks. They did not learn the Turkish language, nor did they attempt to learn Turkish customs.

Europe Discovers Egypt

In 1798, when Egypt was still controlled by the Turks, the French arrived. More than 40,000 French soldiers led by the legendary Napoleon Bonaparte invaded Egypt.

Napoleon had no quarrel with the Egyptian people—or the Turks, for that matter. His enemy was the British. In the late 1700s, Britain controlled trade between Europe and India. Napoleon wanted to establish an overland route to India and take over much of Britain's trade. Such a move would hurt Britain economically and would give France an advantage.

France didn't last long as a threat to the Turks. By 1801 Napoleon and his army had been driven out—by the Turks, with help from the British.

But France had been in Egypt long enough to have an important effect on Egypt's future. No longer was Egypt an overlooked

Napoleon Bonaparte invaded Egypt to weaken British trade.

country in the Middle East. It had, as the French discovered, a wealth of stories to tell.

French historians and scientists brought back some of these stories about pyramids and ancient tombs with mummies. There were important lessons to be learned by archaeologists, people who study ancient cultures.

As the French discovered, Egypt had a wealth of stories to tell.

A large book called *Description de l' Egypte*—really an encyclopedia of the land, history and people of Egypt—was written. Soon all of Europe was buzzing about this unknown ancient land and the fascinating information that could be gathered there.

Muhammad Ali

After the French were driven out of Egypt, the Turks reestablished themselves as the rulers there. In 1805, the head of the Ottoman Empire appointed a former officer in the Turkish army as the local ruler of Egypt.

His name was Muhammad Ali. More than any other individual in the past several centuries, Muhammad Ali had a truly positive effect on Egypt.

Muhammad Ali took full control of the country, down to the smallest detail of his government. As he put it, his aim was to bring Egypt "into the modern world." He began massive building projects and he modernized farms. He introduced a new strain of cotton from India, which could be grown easily by Egyptian farmers. He expanded the irrigation system, using the Nile to enrich more and more of Egypt's farmland.

Under Muhammad Ali, Egyptian students were encouraged to travel to Europe to study. Whatever the students could learn they would bring back to Egypt. This way, Muhammad Ali reasoned, the entire country would benefit from their studies.

Muhammad Ali was also aggressive in making Egypt larger. He expanded the country's borders southward into Sudan. He also pushed the borders east into Saudi Arabia. He was anxious for Egypt to gain power in the Middle East and Africa—and especially to gain control of trade routes.

The history of Egypt during the years between 1805 and 1848 is really the story of Muhammad Ali. He accomplished a great deal for Egypt and for himself. He wished to be so secure that even the Turkish rulers in Istanbul would be unable to unseat him from power. His ambition was fulfilled. After his death, the title of ruler stayed in his family and was handed down several times—just as in a royal family!

The leaders after Muhammad Ali were not all as strong and ambitious as he had been. Some were good; others accomplished very little for Egypt.

A Canal—and Problems

One major event that took place in Egypt during the rule of Muhammad Ali's descendants was so important that it forever changed Egypt's economy and its status in the Middle East.

For many years people had wished for a waterway connecting the Mediterranean Sea and the Red Sea. There would be real advantages in this, especially for merchants and sailors. The route between Britain and its trading partner India would be shortened by a full 6,000 miles!

The waterway was engineered by a Frenchman named Ferdinand de Lesseps. He got permission from the Egyptian ruler in 1854 to undertake the project. De Lesseps reminded the Egyptian government how profitable such a waterway might be. Each ship passing through would have to pay a toll. And in the mid-19th century, there was no shortage of ships willing to do just that.

By 1859, enough money had been raised to begin work on the waterway. Known as the Suez Canal, it was completed in 1869. By previous agreement, the canal would be managed for 99 years by the Suez Canal Company—a combination of Turkish and French investors. (The Ottoman Empire still controlled Egypt.)

But Egypt was swamped with financial problems because of

The Suez Canal

the canal. Heavily in debt and unable to come up with loan payments, Egypt's leaders were glad to be able to sell some of their shares of the Suez Canal Company. They had a ready buyer—Britain!

Britain was very willing to purchase millions of dollars in stock for the company. The British government had a good reason to invest. Because of its long-standing trade agreements with India, British ships were the primary users of the canal. The more involved Britain was in the canal's management, the better off the British economy would be.

Even though Egypt had gained some money in the sale of the stock, it was not enough. The country's economy continued to flounder. And with a weak economy, Egypt's government also grew weaker and less effective.

The British, on the other hand, became a stronger force in Egypt. Their influence in the country spread from the canal to other parts of Egypt's economy. By 1882, British businesspeople had assumed control of almost every part of Egypt's finances. Even though the official rulers of Egypt were appointed by the Ottoman Empire, they were rulers in name only. Now the British controlled Egypt.

Improvements, but with a Price

The British in Egypt worked hard to improve the country. Under British rule Egypt's educational system expanded. Political parties were organized, and a qualified modern army was formed.

The nation's economy also took a turn for the better. For many years under the Turks, Egypt had been exploited for the grain its farmers grew, and much of that had been exported to Turkey. The British knew that Egypt needed a cash crop that would be profitable. Cotton was the crop, and the British helped Egyptian farmers improve their production of it.

The shipping trade grew, and the roads that connected key Egyptian cities were improved. Tourism—something that had never before existed in Egypt—began to flourish. People from around the world wanted to see this remarkable land linked with an ancient past.

But for all the improvements made in Egypt, the country still remained a colony. As the British presence there increased, so did the dissatisfaction of the Egyptian people. The British were not cruel colonial masters, but they were masters nonetheless. Egyptians wanted their freedom—from the Turks, from the British, from any outsiders who tried to control their country. They had been ruled by outsiders for centuries. Enough was enough.

Pressing for Freedom

In the years that followed, Egyptians tried hard to gain their independence. After World War I ended in 1918, there were riots and revolts throughout Egypt. A political group called Wafd was organized to work for Egyptian freedom.

In 1922 the British gave in a little bit. They established what they called the Kingdom of Egypt. British politicians handpicked an Egyptian king—Fuad I—who would rule the country.

But the new kingdom was merely a front. King Fuad, having

King Faud

been chosen by the British, did not represent the Egyptian people. His allegiance was to the British Crown, and Egyptians knew it. The British were still very much a presence in Egypt—their businesses flourished and British troops were stationed there.

The Wafd did not give up. Wafd leaders spoke out tirelessly for independence. In 1936 the British again agreed to give in to Egyptian demands. They granted what they called full independence to Egypt.

But again there were strings attached. The British still controlled the canal. They owned the majority of the stock in the Suez Canal Company, while the French and Turks owned very small portions. The British also kept authority over the Egyptian army. And, most important, British diplomats still controlled Egypt's foreign policy.

Freedom!

It may seem strange that the British could maintain such strict control in a country so far from British shores. But Egypt had a real disadvantage. Despite improvements over the years, the country was still poor. Most of the people were ignorant of politics and the choices available to them.

After World War II, Egyptian leaders became even more vocal about freedom. This was a good time to press the point, too. The British had spent more manpower and money than they had wanted to in fighting in Egypt. They were now unwilling to take on a fight with an unruly colony in the Middle East.

Anti-British feelings in Egypt had reached a new height.

King Farouk

People were angry with King Farouk, who had taken the throne after Fuad died. Farouk's greed and his lavish lifestyle infuriated Egyptians, many of whom were living in poverty.

In 1952 there was a military coup, or uprising, against King Farouk. The leader of the coup was an officer named Gamal Abdel Nasser. The coup was bloodless—King Farouk had known about the uprising and had fled to safety in Italy. When it was over, Egypt had a new ruler—Gamal Nasser. And for the first time since ancient times, Egypt was a free, self-governing nation.

EGYPT AND THE MIDDLE EAST CONFLICT

Unfortunately for the Egyptians, their country's problems could not be solved by independence alone. In fact, many of Egypt's most difficult problems arose after it broke its colonial ties with Britain. These difficulties had little to do with Britain. They had to do with the other nations in the Middle East and the growing tensions among them.

Beginning with Palestine

Much of the friction in the Middle East began over a piece of land known as Palestine. Palestine is located to the east and north of Egypt and the Sinai Peninsula. Although Palestine has never been a self-ruling, independent nation, it has an important and ancient history.

Like Egypt and other Arab nations in the Middle East, Palestine was once part of the Ottoman Empire. Palestine also fell under British control as the power of the Turks lessened.

But Palestine was different from other Arab nations. It was considered holy by two very different religions. The vast majority of people living in Palestine were Arab Muslims. They valued Palestine because it was the site of the city of Jerusalem. And Jerusalem was the place from which the prophet Muhammad had risen to heaven.

There were also thousands of Jews living in Palestine. While they were no longer the majority . . Palestine, their attachment to the place was far older than the Arabs'. Palestine was the promised land that God had once pledged to early Jewish leaders such as Moses and Abraham. Even though few Jews had lived in Palestine for many centuries, they still believed it to be theirs by God's plan.

Whose Land?

Between World War I and World War II, many British-held lands in the Middle East were demanding independence. Palestine was among them.

But there were questions that needed to be answered: What sort of country would Palestine be? Would it belong to the Arab Muslims, who formed the majority? Or would it belong to the Jews, who claimed it as their birthright?

The British were unwilling to give a straight answer to either side. On one hand, they assured the Arabs that they would do nothing to upset the life they had in Palestine. On the other, the British understood that the Jews were persecuted by many people around the world. It was understandable that the Jews wanted their own homeland. So the British promised that they would take care of the Jews.

"It was diplomatic foolishness," says one historian. "There was simply no way that the British could live up to both promises. By keeping one they would automatically break the other."

The Deciding Factor

The deciding factor in the fate of Palestine was the treatment of the Jews by Germany during World War II. Adolf Hitler and his Nazi party considered the Jews enemies of the

German state. The solution, for Hitler, was to kill as many of them as he could.

Jewish men, women and children were rounded up and placed in death camps. There they were shot, tortured or killed in specially built gas chambers. In all, more than six million Jews—about one-third of all the Jews in the world—were exterminated by the Nazis.

At the end of World War II, American, British and French forces saw these death camps for the first time. Mass graves containing thousands of Jewish people were uncovered. As reports of these atrocities—known as the Holocaust—became public, the world was horrified.

Many survivors of the Holocaust were even more determined that they should have a homeland. "Never again," wept a man who had lost his wife and three of his children to the gas chambers. "The Jews will never be treated this way again."

Many people in the world agreed. The Jews had suffered so much. It seemed logical that they *should* have a land of their own. So popular opinion was strongly pro-Jewish.

The Partition and War

Just as Britain had allowed Egypt its freedom after the war, the British government was anxious to be rid of the problem of Palestine. How could they deal with the Palestinian Arabs who were the majority in Palestine?

British officials turned the problem over to the newly formed United Nations. It was hoped that this international lawmaking body could find the answers.

The UN's decision was to partition, or divide, Palestine.

More than half of the country was given to the Jews. The rest was given to the Arabs. Jerusalem, because of its special significance to both, was placed under international control.

The Arabs were furious. They angrily spoke out against the plan and vowed revenge. A civil war broke out between Arabs and Jews in Palestine, and the Jews won. Now in control of the vast majority of Palestinian land, the Jews renamed it Israel.

Some Arabs stayed in Israel, but most left. They were unwilling to remain in a place governed by Jews. "It was our land, our farms, our schools," said one Arab woman angrily. "But we are a people without a country now. We can migrate to another Arab state, but it will not be our own. We have been robbed."

Egypt's Response

Throughout the Middle East, Arabs were angry at what had happened to their fellow Arabs in Palestine. In 1948 Egypt was one of four Arab nations to send army units to Israel to fight the Jews.

But the Jewish soldiers had the upper hand. They were organized and better armed than the Arabs. Too, they were fighting for their existence as a new state, and that gave them the determination to win.

Egypt's loss was hard for its people to take. Egyptians were ashamed that their nation had been defeated by the brand-new state of Israel. They blamed the humiliating defeat on their king, Farouk. King Farouk was already the object of scorn because of his spending and the corruption of his advisers. It was not surprising, then, when Nasser and his fellow officers staged the coup that got rid of Farouk in 1952.

Gamal Abdel Nasser

Egyptian soldiers captured by the French during the Suez War

Fighting Israel

Nasser set goals in many areas—the economy, agriculture, industry and long-overdue social reforms. But by far the most challenging goal was that of uniting the Arab nations. He promised Egyptians that "the Egyptian people and our Arab brothers will not rest until we liberate Palestine."

He was not successful in that goal. He did, however, go to war on more than one occasion with the Arab enemy, Israel.

In 1956 Nasser took control of the Suez Canal from the British and the French. He saw no reason why those two nations should continue to get money that the Egyptian people needed to make improvements in their own country.

Nasser's actions angered Britain and France. Both of those nations joined with Israel in 1956 to attack Egypt. Egypt retaliated by not allowing French and British ships to use the canal—thus cutting off those nations' ties with the East.

The Suez War, as it was called, did not last long. Under pressure from the United Nations—and the United States in particular—the three nations withdrew their armies from Egypt. Nasser, in the eyes of the Arab world, was something of a hero. He had stood up to both European powers and the hated Israelis and had not backed down.

A Dangerous Buildup

Through the next decade, Egypt built itself into a major power in the Middle East. The Soviet Union offered to supply Egypt with weapons and other technology. At the same time, Israel was being armed by the United States. The large Jewish population in America put heavy pressure on government leaders to support the Jewish state.

A New Leader

But even though Egypt continued to get state-of-the-art weapons from the Soviet Union, it was unable to do what Nasser had promised—to "liberate Palestine." In 1967 Israel became the aggressor. In an unexpected strike, Israel destroyed almost the entire Egyptian air force while it was on the ground.

The Six-Day War, as it was called, was a disaster for Arabs in the Middle East. Not only were they unable to cripple the Israeli army and drive the Jews from Palestine, but it was dangerous for them to even try! Egypt lost all of its lands east of the Suez Canal in that short war.

Nasser was heartbroken that Egypt had been defeated so soundly. He even offered to resign, but the Egyptian people were loyal to him. He ruled Egypt until he died of a heart attack in 1970.

A Plan for Peace

Nasser's vice president took over when he died. His name was Anwar al-Sadat. Sadat was eager for Egypt to reclaim the territory it had lost in the war with Israel. After rebuilding Egypt's army and air force, Sadat ordered his troops to attack the lands east of the Suez Canal, the Sinai, in 1973.

Anwar al-Sadat

The Camp David treaty was a remarkable step toward peace in the Middle East.

The attack was a success. Egypt regained its lands in the Sinai—and its pride. Now in a position of strength, Sadat felt he could negotiate with Israeli leaders. Could peace be worked out?

One person who hoped so was U.S. President Jimmy Carter. Like other world leaders, Carter knew how dangerous the hostilities in the Middle East could be. He was anxious for Israel and Egypt to make a move toward peace. If they did, Carter felt sure the other nations of the Middle East might follow.

In 1978 Carter invited Sadat and Israeli Prime Minister Menachem Begin to his presidential getaway at Camp David in Maryland. There the three hammered out an agreement that would pave the way to peace. No more were Egypt and Israel in a state of war and distrust. They would work together toward a lasting peace.

The Camp David treaty, as it was known, was hailed around the world as a remarkable achievement. Carter was respected as a peacemaker, and Sadat and Begin were congratulated for putting aside past quarrels.

Cold Shoulder from the Arab World

Not everyone was pleased about the Camp David treaty. The rest of the Arab world looked at Sadat as something of a traitor.

"He has sold Egypt and his Arab brothers," said a student from Syria. "We looked to Egypt as strength against the threat of these [Jewish] people. But Sadat wants instead to dance with them!"

Many Arabs agreed. They felt that Sadat had betrayed them all—especially the Palestinians who still had no home. Yasir Arafat was the leader of the Palestine Liberation Organization (PLO). The group has often resorted to terrorism against Israel. Arafat called on Arabs everywhere to unite against Sadat.

Only Sudan supported Egypt. The governments of Jordan and Saudi Arabia were careful not to take sides. But Syria, Iraq, Algeria and Libya condemned Egypt and Sadat. They called Egypt "an enemy of Arab unity and of Islam."

Sadat was hated by many Egyptians, too. As he stood watching a military parade in Cairo on October 6, 1981, soldiers in the parade turned and fired at him. He was killed, and his assassins quickly gave themselves up.

They were Egyptians, but they claimed they were "loyal Muslims, which Sadat was not." They believed that they had been justified in their action, for Sadat had made peace with an enemy of Islam. He had failed, they thought, to be true to the Arab world.

An assasin fires his machine gun at point-blank range, killing Anwar al-Sadat.

THE CHALLENGE TO MUBARAK

Hosni Mubarak was Sadat's vice president. He took over as president after Sadat was assassinated. Mubarak's presidency has had many challenges.

One of Mubarak's major accomplishments has been to smooth relations with other Arab nations. Mubarak's views are similar to Sadat's. However, he has been more diplomatic and less outspoken than Sadat about a number of controversial issues. Because of this, he has been able to strengthen ties with other Arab nations. At the same time, Egypt has been able to hold fast to the terms of the Camp David treaty.

The Persian Gulf War

A major challenge occurred during the 1991 Persian Gulf War. Mubarak spoke out against the aggression of Saddam Hussein, as did some other Arab leaders. As an ally of the United States (since the signing of the Camp David treaty, Egypt receives billions of dollars each year in aid), Egypt agreed to participate in the war. More than 40,000 Egyptian soldiers took part in the war, positioned on Kuwait's border.

But although many Arabs condemned Saddam Hussein's taking of Kuwait, they were uneasy about Egyptians fighting Iraqis.

Egyptian gunners arrive in Saudi Arabia, part of a larger force that fought against Iraq.

"I do not like it, this Arab fighting Arab," said one Egyptian woman who had two sons in the army. "It seems wrong, like it is against nature somehow. Hussein has made a bad mistake, but maybe Egypt is making another. What if the war spreads, and our whole part of the world is the battlefield? Will all the Arabs be fighting all the Arabs? Who can win?"

Fighting the Arabs was a difficult decision for the Egyptian people.

Egyptian youths burn a wood effigy of Saddam Hussein.

41

Tens of thousands of Muslims kneel in prayer.

42

Threats to a Peaceful Future

As it turned out, the war did not become a large Middle East war. And some Egyptians believe the war helped their economy. Because of Egypt's participation, about half of its foreign debt will be erased—from $50 billion to $25 billion by 1994.

But severe economic problems still grip the country. The population is growing rapidly, and there are too few jobs for the people who need them. Inflation is growing, and people's salaries can't keep up with the rising prices.

The threat of terrorism and other violence grows daily. It is not just the PLO or other extremist Arab groups that are threats. More and more, religious groups in Egypt are responsible for shootings, bombings and killings.

Fundamentalist Muslims—those who hold strictly to the teachings of Muhammad—have spoken out against the government of Egypt. They say that Mubarak's plans to modernize Egypt are a threat to the Muslim way of life. They say, too, that Mubarak's continued ties with Israel and the countries of the West are against the teachings of Islam.

Mubarak has said publicly that he wants politics and religion to be separate. He considers himself a good Muslim, but he sees the danger in using religion as a basis of governing Egypt.

"I don't want headaches," said Mubarak in 1990. "I would like to build a country, not cause reasonable people to fight one another."

President Mubarak waves to the people during his first public appearance after Kuwait was liberated.

In the months and years ahead, it will be interesting to see whether Mubarak and other Egyptian leaders can rebuild their country. Or will religious battles cause more anguish and sorrow in a land that has already seen too much of both?

FACTS ABOUT EGYPT

Capital: Cairo

Population: 54.7 million

Form of government: Republic

Official language: Arabic

Unit of money: Pound

Major religions: Sunni Moslem, Islam, Coptic Christianity

Chief products: cotton, corn, rice, wheat, sugarcane, iron, steel,
      textiles, chemicals, cement

Glossary

Arab world *The lands inhabited by people originally from the land called Arabia.*

archaeologist *A person who studies the remains of ancient civilizations.*

Byzantine *The Eastern part of the Roman Empire.*

Coptic Christianity *The belief that Jesus was totally divine and not human.*

coup *A military takeover of a government.*

fundamentalist *A person who is very strict about his or her religious beliefs.*

Holocaust *The murder of approximately six million Jews by the Nazis during World War II.*

Islam *The religion practiced by Muslims; Islam is the official religion of Egypt.*

Muslims *People who practice the faith called Islam.*

partition *To divide or segment an area.*

pharaohs *The rulers of ancient Egypt.*

Wafd *A political group formed after World War I and dedicated to working for Egyptian independence.*

Index

Libya 36

Mediterranean Sea 10, 18
Middle East 8, 13, 15, 17,
  18, 23, 25, 26, 28, 31, 32,
  35, 43
Mubarak, Hosni 6, 7, 8, 38,
  43, 44
Muhammad 13, 25, 43
Muhammad Ali 17, 18
Muslims 7, 8, 11, 13, 14,
  25, 26, 36, 43

Nasser, Gamal Abdel 24,
  28, 31, 32
Nazi Germany 26, 27
Nile River 6, 10, 17

Ottoman Empire 14, 17, 18,
  20, 25

Palestine 25, 26, 27, 28, 31,
  32, 36
Palestine Liberation Orga-
  nization (PLO) 36, 43
Persian Gulf War 38
Persians 10

Red Sea 18
Roman Empire 10, 11, 13

Saudi Arabia 17, 36
Sinai Penninsula 25, 27
Six-Day War 32
Soviet Union 31, 32
Sudan 17, 36
Suez Canal 18, 31, 32
Suez Canal Company 18, 20,
  23
Suez War 31
Syria 36

Turkey 14, 17, 18, 21, 23, 25

United Nations 27, 31
United States 6, 7, 31, 32, 38

Wafd 21, 23
Western Empire 11
World War I 21, 26
World War II 23, 26, 27